Get I.T.! Start A Career In Information Technology

SADANAND PUJARI

Published by SADANAND PUJARI, 2024.

Table of Contents

Copyright 1

About 2

Introduction 3

The 4 Ws & 1 H 4

The Who? 5

Focus 7

Do you? 8

What? 9

Information System Management Areas 10

The 4 Areas of an Information System Management 11

The Where 14

Guide into ITS for Students/Graduates 16

Guide into ITS for Students/Graduates 2 19

Guide into ITS for Professionals 21

Extra Motivation 22

How? 23

Information System Management Starting Points 24

Starting Point in Networking Career Training 25

Starting Point in Programming Career Training.......................... 27

Starting Point in Software Career Training................................ 28

The Why 30

Examples of my preferred beginners training with career path 31

IT Networking Career Path for Beginners..................................... 32

IT Programing Career Path for Beginners 34

IT Software Career Path for Beginners 36

Copyright

Copyright © 2024 by **SADANAND PUJARI**

All rights reserved. No part of this book may be reproduced, scanned, or distributed in any printed or electronic form without permission. Please do not participate in or encourage piracy of copyrighted materials in violation of the author's rights. Purchase only authorised editions.

Get I.T.! Start A Career In Information Technology

How To Find An Entry-Level Job In I.T. Without Formal Education Or Work History

First Edition: Jun 2024

Book Design by **SADANAND PUJARI**

About

Are you considering launching a career in information technology, but don't know how and where to start? This Book is created for you to answer your questions, and also will have the opportunity to ask a mentor who has been in the IT industry your questions.

This Book or knowledge transfer like I like to call it explores entry level training or serves as a guide to you to know what is available within the growing and lucrative IT industry. In today's world, businesses require information technology, or IT, to remain competitive and provide the best products and services to customers. As more and more businesses discover ways to use technology to their benefit, demand for trained and specialized IT professional's demands grows every day.

The Book is written in plain, clear language, to make it easy for anyone to follow. No prior background or education in I.T. is required. The intended audience for the Book is absolute beginners looking to start a new career in I.T.

Introduction

Hi. Are you looking to start a career in the IT industry? If you're looking to start a career in the I.T. industry, I welcome you to this book. Before you take this Book, I would like to walk you through some decisive questions that you can answer for yourself. You can use that at the top of this Book is what? First, do you know that there are three steps into starting an IT career? Number one, get training in it if you were to pass on the interview. And number three, doing the actual job. In my years of experience, I've seen people passing the interview at the end of the day, the starting job, and they get fired.

But I'm not going to be talking about doubt in this Book. This Book is going to be focusing on the training that I teach here. Everybody knows that for you to start a career, to feel, you have to get through it. But the actual question is, do you know the training to take? Do you know the starting point? How do you stop? These are the questions that we are going to be construed in this Book. So if you are a student or a professional, I welcome you to take this Book and hopefully this will help you in your journey on how to start an IT career.

The 4 Ws & 1 H

Welcome back. In this Book, I'm going to be using the four W's on one each formula in this knowledge transfer like I like to call it. I'm going to be using the photo, please, out of the fathomless formula for getting the complete story out on our subject.

Which one H. And what is our subject? How to start an I.T. career or where do you start from? What are the four W's on one H formula that we're going to be using is going to be the whole. The what, the where? The Y. And the Al. This is going to be the formula that we are going to be using in this book. To get you started on how to start an I.T. career.

The Who?

Let's talk about the WHO. The whole year. He's. Always transferring this knowledge to you in this Book. And how we are transferring this knowledge to you on how to start your career in I.T.. And the question is, what qualifies me to be that person? I started my career as a computer technician where I studied computer engineering. I have 19 years of experience in the high tech industry. And let me walk you through the roadmap of my career so far in the IT industry. Started my career as a computer technician studying computer engineering in school. Then I went into history for a diploma in information system management. I also took training information. Business management.

Suddenly, my career as a computer technician after my diploma in information system management. I became a Web developer where I developed a couple of websites for businesses. Then I switched my career from being a Web developer. I became a SQL data analyst. Where I get trained in the Microsoft sequel Cassava. And I had a successful career a little bit. In that environment where I also worked. And then I switch my car from being a school. Data analyst into becoming a business analyst. As a business analyst at Wolf, organizations had to walk with a requirement gallery's translations of requirements. And after my career as a business analyst, I moved up the ladder.

I became an SNP consultant. We are also up to the certifications in that area. As an ACP consultant. That moves up the ladder. I became an SRP project manager, which is what I currently do today. Over the past two years of my experience in the industry, I've also been a trainer. Trained individuals on how to start their career in I.T. and also train them in some S.O.P applications. I have several individuals that I've been successful in the field. And also, over the years, I've been a mentor to college students on how to start a career in the outfield. So I will tell you that these are the fees that I believe qualifies me to put this cost together, to say how and to guide you on where. You can start your career in I.T..

Let's talk about who is receiving this knowledge. If you will listen to me, you might be a student or you might be a professional. And you are the one receiving or who is going to be receiving this knowledge. And the reason why you're receiving this knowledge is because you're looking. To go into the I.T. industry. And I'm going to have some questions for you. In the after chapter of this chapter. But before that question. Let's talk about. Who is this knowledge about? We are no. This knowledge is all about information technology. And if you right right now listen to this chapter is because there have been several informations, are there, about this individual? I t. Which is something we are going to be breaking down in this Book about this individual ELITE. And from a beginner standpoint, for you to really understand what an item is. And what you have to do.

Focus

There are two types of individuals that want to start, and I t. What a college or university student. All graduates and two assistant professions. In this case, this Book is going to be tailored to these two types of individuals. A student or graduate or an assistant professional looking to start a career in I.T..

Do you?

Hi. In the last chapter of the Hu. I said before you decide to take this Book. I would like to leave you with these four questions. The question is do you ask yourself questions? No one. Do you know the four areas of the Hiti career path? Number two, do you have what it takes? And number three, do you know how to decide where to start from? In the fall. Do you know what you already have? If you are successfully able to answer this question, I guess this cost is not for you. But. You can take this Book for knowledge. But if you are not successfully able to answer this question. I will recommend this Book to you. Because at the end of this Book, I believe that you will be able to answer these four questions. To a nearby youdecide. And for you to know how you can start your career in the I.T. industry.

What?

Hi, welcome back. In this chapter, we're going to be talking about what is an I.T. information technology? The definition of information technology is the use of computers to store data and information. Everybody knows this. Even a layman can give with this defamation. But as you go into the ITIC area, all looking to go into the Itakura, the world for you is not what is an I.T.. The real question is. The want is actually. What goes on, I.T., individual or exparte do? I think individual experts walk to either build, monitor, manage, support, computer networks, programs. Otherwise, I softworks within an organization. That is what I expect. Over the years of my experience, I've seen when you Axum individuals in the IT industry, what do they do? He responded by saying, I do it.

So say I walk in it. And a lot of people say, I want to do it, but I don't really tell you about these functions or break things down like this. So the second thing I want you to understand in this chapter these days. When you say you are going into the and you decide on the training that you want to embark on, whatever I.T. training that you gain today, what the training is actually doing or what knowledge is the training actually transferring to you? Is it either how to build, how to monitor, how to manage and how to support these areas of I.T.. In network programs, Arthua, or software for any organizations that are out there.

Information System Management Areas

Welcome back. In this chapter, we're going to be talking about understanding information system management areas. If you have made it far away from me to the world of information technology. In my earlier chapter. I talked about it. My knowledge and information system management. What information technology is an umbrella? That covers the entire area. Of its components. All we can call it. It's a.. Of function. There are four areas if you're looking to go into the eyes of fear, you must understand these. I've seen the majority of folks do it. They said they walk in it. But the question is, what area of I.T. Do they really want it? I see so many student individuals on proficiency, they want to go into I.T.. And when you ask them the question. What part of it are you looking at? To pursue.

They really did not have an idea. All they say is, I want to do T. So in this chapter, let's quickly look at the four areas of I.T. information technology and information technology. We have. Networking. Programming Hadaway. And software. In networking, there are different functionalities in programming that have different functionality, and in hardware, they have different functionalities and software. They have different functionality as well. And in this chapter, we are going to be talking about these functionalities and breaking things down so that you can understand what it means. To say I do want to walk in and it or if somebody sees I walk in and you are able to hold a conversation and ask them what area of it are you into?

The 4 Areas of an Information System Management

Let's talk about the four areas of information system management in this chapter. I'm going to be breaking this down for areas of understanding. The first one, networking. This is the area of I.T. wet transporting and exchanging data between nodes over a shared medium of information system. To simplify these, the networking part of information system management is the part that handles communication between computers. When computers communicate together through any medium, that communication is the networking of this computer that enables them to be able to communicate with each other. In today's world, we have several ways computers communicate with each other, either on the premises or in the cloud Internet intranet.

It doesn't really matter as long as it deals with the communications of computers. Every individual is an expert in these areas of I.T. They are classified under the networking area of information system management and Chavira, such as network engineer, network administrator. Etsy is part of this area of I.T. and you can develop and become a subject matter expert and also obtain certifications in this area, such as Ishani. S. C. A. GCT seekamp compassion, a compassion airplus, just to name a few. Even in networking these days, you also have cloud computing. But as we go into this Book, I will be here to break this down. Number two, programI.

This is the area of information system management where computers of this ward driven by programs, abuse software applications are developed, computer programmers are the builders of the computer world. Developing Naqoura in programI is to be able to write computer codes. There are several computer codes out there. Such computer codes are Sureshot C++, Python and Caresser. You can pursue it. These are software engineers and also people call them Java developers. Certifications can also be uptime as well. In this area of information system management. Number three, either way in my head, your chapter of introduction, I started my career as a computer technician.

I was an off-world individual when I was pursuing a career. This is the area of information system management where fixing tangible computers, devices such as personal industrial computers, industrial printers, physical Sarvas, EDC, developing Paduan, Odwa, such as I.T. technicians. When I started my career, you can also classify me back then as an I.T. technician. You also have careers like I.T. administrator, decks of support engineers, I.T., ATEX, I.T. managers, EDC, Wasta goals, and then a certification that can also be obtained in this area of I.T.. So if you are somebody that is handy and you are looking to get into the workforce, you might also consider starting your career path in either way. But as we go forward in this Book, I'm also going to be discussing some options for every individual. And lastly, we're going to be talking about software in today's world.

This is the area where I specialize now in software. This is the era of it. We're focusing on soccer applications that have been built by developer or developer organizations that specialize in application development and computer programs to help light businesses to small businesses perform the day to day tax on all business processes. That is the area of software developing a career in software is to become a subject matter expert in knowing how to use these software applications to add to the industry. It's Taylor's turn to strive for such software. Applications are ERP software auditing software block software, database software and certifications can also be obtained in these areas. Majority of professionals found herself in this area of information software management. And as we go into this Book, I'm going to be breaking these areas down to our understanding and where we can then be able to decide where to start our journey from either as a student or as a professional.

The Where

Let's come to the weather. Welcome to this chapter. There are several places you can learn it, no doubt, and these places are platforms that give you access to the ELITE area of the family that you decide to explore. These places all spring off from these three, whereas one from your college or your universities to from EXPRESS professionals and three from your job employers. Let's take from your college. If you are a student or a graduate, you must have learned something from your college or university. Not everybody is fortunate enough to major in I.T. curriculums. As a matter of fact, 70 percent or 80 percent of students major in I.T. field, which is part of what we have in our book in this Book, to leverage what you have today and how you can jump start a career in I.T..

Number two, you can also learn from expert professionals, someone like myself. Aspirin's professional in today's world, I've created Books to put on different platforms. But you must be able to also understand the part of it that you want to learn so that you can find the right express professionals that you can go with number three from your job or your employers. Yes, you can learn from your job or your employers. And blessing to these Warde also provide Portas where the employees can learn. But how do you leverage this opportunity is to understand and know where to start from. Only then will you be able to utilize all these three ways that you can learn it. I will be providing the resources that place platforms that you can go to, where you can get a list of professionals. You can take training from. And if you have any questions, please feel free to drop a comment or a message to the instructor.

Guide into ITS for Students/Graduates

The first step that we are going to talk about. Welcome back to this chapter. In this chapter, I'm going to be talking about a guide to information system management for students and graduates. You're indecisive college or university majors now? Yes. They provide you with a range of specialties, skills in the areas of information system management. Most often when I go online to do research before I create this Book. I see. There Is a lot of information out there. Well, the truth is all this information is scattered around some banks just to. Publicize. But in this Book, I want to take out all the noises and go straight to the point. Top seven, indecisive college or university majors. I want to start with that for the student audience that is going to be taking this Book. Number one, psychology.

You can learn two wars also stored in data types of industry data, how data are derived, how data behave and where is this data stored. A student with psychology looking to go into the IT industry. Yes, it is doable with your background. All you have to do is to understand and to know and to decide what I feared. Do you want to get trained so that you can put your resume out there and start looking for that position and also understand how to interview for this position? So if you have a degree or you have a major in psychology. Yes, it is doable. These can make you become a data psychologist. Best word for it is data science. In today's what is a new path of career is called data science. People

OSAT colleges are great for these types of. Field. Or you can also become a data analyst.

This would be the study of databases you already stored in the behavior of humans. It's the same thing every individual in the data feeds in one way or the harder they study the behaviors of data. Number two, economics. Yes. If you are measured or you have majored in economics, you can get into the itiR. You can lean towards data or pricing. Fortune 500 companies in today's world have a lot of data. They want to be able to put products out there with different costs. They want to understand your customer base. So all you need to do as an economics person is also to understand the touch of these industry leaders. Pricing data is and how they drive and drive as well. These can make you become an economic analyst. Data size.

Data analyst as well. This would be the story of the stunning potential outcomes of economics or financial decisions for organizations. You can go out there and search for this job. Understand this job and look into the requirements. And you'll be able to find how you can have your own needs with what you have. Non-military Brisas administrations. If you have majored in Business Administration as a student or as a graduate. You can lean towards also starring in one or two software applications that help organizations thrive on automated business processes. These can make you become a business or functional system analyst, business process analyst or business analyst. Even business analysts. This would be the study of guardroom, evaluating and integrating requirements for organizations applications. So if you have a degree in business administration.

Yes, you can start your career in I.T. by leveraging the right resources for yourself.

Guide into ITS for Students/ Graduates 2

Let's look at number four. Phil Ellisville. Not nothing, actually, that filled that up outside Milson practices sources at signs. We have people doing health education. We have people who are social workers that are looking to go into the industry. You can link to us also stored in data or applications. Software's in the health industry. There are several applications of software that I've been using in the industry today, such as EMR systems. These Gumee can be calm, health or data system analyst Aswad IMAO systems and others such as Epic, Seiner, Fastnet, Etsy. These are a few lists of earmark systems that show them. This would be the study of health care systems or data environments.

When I was a second data analyst, I was in a field, but I was walking with health status and that is where I got to lay these like patients. Data, patient insurance data. So there are a lot of opportunities in the I.T. industry for S.K Field, major people that do not have a law degree. You can jump right in to start a career in I.T. field. Communications or mass communications? You can lean towards also stored in how computers are connected to each other. If you have majored in any of these fields of communications, you can learn how computers communicate, computer notes, and computer networking. You can start a career by becoming a communication analyst or data communication on at least on network made or specialist.

This would be the study of computer mediums of communications. No cease marketing. Majority of students and graduates are in the market and see it, and they are looking into how they can study it. You can lean towards also studying how social media walks on the end of the backend and what data they have in today's world. There are a lot of social media. Yeah, a lot of mobile apps. There are a lot of applications online in the Web environment. A lot of companies are looking to market the product, the services. These can make you become an Internet marketer. Social media, marketing and marketing analysts. This would be the study of data being collected through social media and customer up, which is. There are several ways you can leverage your marketing degree today in the I.T. field.

And you just need to find the right resources and tools whenever you get to this full potential. And the last number seven, Buyology, Maharaji is one of the top seven undecided seats majors in the university today. And I've come across a lot of students in this environment. You can link lean towards also starting about data analytics. Remember, one of my chapters I said is driven by different types of industries. And as a biologist, you can become a medical or a pharmaceutical research analyst, you can also become a clinical research analyst with what you've got. This will be the study of helping the industry towards quality control compliances and decision making patients and tries. But you just need to know the right tools. So that. If you have any comment or any message or any question for the Instructor Chiffre to ask if you are a student or graduate or an individual that is taking this call.

Guide into ITS for Professionals

Welcome back. In this chapter, I'm going to be talking about a guide into information system management for professionals and orders in the past session. We've talked about the guiding information system management for students and graduates that probably might have taken, you know, top of the seven indecisive majors in colleges or universities that are looking to go into the ITF. Here in this chapter, I'm going to be talking about the professionals or the law related I.T. degrees. Oh, you don't have a college or university degree. And everyone else. Yeah, also careers that you can pursue as a profession for beginners. I always like to mentor my be Guinness to start with either a business analyst, I.T. analyst, system analyst, data analyst, network analyst, or CECO data analyst for professionals.

They are not a bunch of. Covid asked if I had bought these seas, Korea for me. I think these are the best recommendations for a starting point for professionals. Then you can take this step further in your career. In one of my past chapters, I talked about the why, part of the why ease as an artist or individual. You need to be a long time, so full of beginner's guide for a long time. These are my six recommendations for professionals.

Extra Motivation

OK. I like to give some motivation as we go deep down into this book. I want you to know that you have to always be part of the reason behind your always being an innovation, career success and innovation is all for you. You know, peace, freedom, professional creativity, happiness and growth. You might have your own reasons why you want to start a career in I.T. It might be for professionalism, for financial freedom, for creativity, happiness or growth. Either way, one thing I want you to understand is pursuing a career in the. Yet you always have to be a part of the reason behind your own sources and your innovations.

How?

The last in the formula in this chapter, we are going to be talking about the owl, which is the last. And as we begin to come to an end of these calls, let's take a look at the last comment. The eHow is a major challenge for a lot of individuals because of Savas Catelli information being passed around from the Internet and friends of folks without guidance and a starting point. Many individuals want to go into the ELITE and many ulcerated Johnny Bodia lost. Because of Scotter, the information either from the Internet, friends or false. In one of my chapters, I mention that I am a mentor, and these are the majority of issues that I have in this common book. So if you have any questions, feel free to message the instructor. And I'll be glad to respond to your question if you find yourself in the situation.

Information System Management Starting Points

In this chapter, back again, what are the information system management starting points? We are going to be talking about a starting point here, which is the focus of this book. The starting point in the information system, management in networking and programI hardware and software. How do I start? Where do I start from? How do I know this is the right fit for me? These are the questions that we are about to answer as we go for them.

Starting Point in Networking Career Training

Hi. In this chapter I'm going to be talking about recommending a starting point in networking career training. If you have decided to go into networking as a career choice in I.T., my preferred recommendations are for beginners training for you to start with learning Microsoft Office Sutt Tools. The Microsoft Office system. Choose a kid, monitor and choose for I.T.. Experts and these tools and threes, the Microsoft Word, Microsoft, Excel, PowerPoint. And there are several levels to these suits. You have the beginners intermediate at expert level looking into going to the ELITE. You don't have to go to the expert level in landing a Microsoft suit. You can get to an intermediate level in these tools.

G-suit, a Jemez suit, a version of the Jimmi worn for office is still the same thing. When you go to the G.M., should you have chevre? All the tools that you can leverage out there, including Spreadsheet and presentations. The one thing you need to know is that you don't have to lend the two ideas in time. All you have to do is speak one and lend just one. And my recommendation would be the maps of the office. So choose because with one, you will be able to function in the order. The mess begins as training that I'll recommend you take. If you are thinking about going into talking, a career in I.T. is going to start with compassion.

A, they will give you the foundation of networking in the IT industry. When you finish, they come to a I will recommend you go for content applause. They come to Airplus, give you the update on the AI and also other functionalities that you need to know about these beginners training in an Iraqi arrangement. I will say start Microsoft Office to come to a and come to blows when you are done. You can then proceed to the advanced networking learning the server environment and career paths in the advanced networking learning that you can embark on in the advanced learning. Where I've come to an end is a plus, we have come to our security. Plus, we have cyber security. We have Amazon Web services enabling acts.

You are Microsoft Cloud Service, Azazel, and you have all these clever networking platforms or networking tools that I have. But like I said, my recommendation in these calls as a beginner looking to go into the IT industry is to start with either the Microsoft Office shooters or G-suit and make sure you take that, come to a and come to airplus training. And that will give you a head start into developing a career in the networking environment, in the information system management industry.

Starting Point in Programming Career Training

In this chapter, I'm going to be talking about my recommended starting point in my programming career. It was said, programmers are the beauties of applications, writing codes. If this is an area of the information system management that you want to pursue, my beginner's training recommendation is to start with HTML. JavaScript, and she says these are very important. Applications, according to that, you can learn. When I was three, with my information system management diploma, I became a Web developer. I run a small business consulting today. I don't have to write the code. I don't have to be on the website today because I have people doing that. But one thing I can do is also to validate their work.

And how am I able to do that because I have the foundations of an A.M. JavaScript exercise. They begin our starting point for programs. My recommendation will be to take the HTML JavaScript training. They do this training. You have the beginners, the intermediate and the expert level. I will recommend you get to the intermediate level. Then if you want to advance your programming learning, then you can take these advanced programming languages. Java, C, sharp C++, PSP, E.S.P about SeQual and Python. There are several programming languages out there that you can learn. However, if you don't have the foundation, you would not have a grasp of what it means to code. So I will come back again. My recommendation is to start with HTML, JavaScript and SHESAYS.

Starting Point in Software Career Training

In this session, let's talk about my recommendation, starting point for software career training. Yes, I do understand that I skip hardware. I want to focus on how to start a career in I.T. for the majority of folks. Students, all professionals. My beginner's recommendation, training first to start a career in the software area of information system management is to take computer training, computer training or compassion training. The reason I say computer training, I am a trainer myself and now there are several people that want to go into the IT industry that don't even know the basic things. The basic navigation is on the computer or the laptop. They kind of open a folder. They don't even know how to put a thumb drive on their laptop. They don't even know how to look for a file, how to share a file on their computers.

These are basic things that you have to learn. If you are looking to go into the industry, most especially in the software area of information system management. Number two, you also have to land the Microsoft Office to use, because these are managerial tools that you are going to be using for your data, the functionality I want. And number three, collaboration tools. What do I mean by collaboration? Tee's Collaboration tools are tools that are used for file sharing or working within a team application, such as Chod, Balts, Slack's teams, WebEx, zoom. These are collaborations with TS G-suit. These are collaborations to confluence. These are collaboration tools, ticketing systems. These are collaboration teams.

You need to learn one of these tools to leverage in order to be able to get yourself started in the software Padam career. Then the advice of learning, once you are done with a beginner's ease, you then need to look to learn a computer application. That was a starting point, and software is you have to learn one or two software applications. It's not enough to say you want to go into I.T. with hard understanding or without peak in an application that an industry is using or a company is using to put out there. So the first recommendation, advanced recommendation, is you can either learn a computer relation, relationship management system or application. They are Savara customer relationship management systems that are out there.

You can either learn an enterprise resource planning system, applications that are out, that all you can learn a database system on applications that are there, or you can also learn an industry solution system tailored towards an industry that I have. I'm going to be putting the resources you have for at least a customer relationship management system, enterprise resource planning systems, database systems, and also some industrial solutions systems that you can pick from and you can look for resources out there and you will be able to take training in them. Then you are on your way to a starting point in pursuing a career in the software area, the information system management.

The Why

The Y. The wife is simply asking yourself a question. Protecting the future of your career is an act of embracing connectivity and change without fear. Our lives are increasingly being connected to the world of information system management today. You need to start now by leveraging resources and to argue that either why we are in search of how to start a career in I.T. in these chapters. Two points, I want you to take your weight. You. Embracing connectivity and change without fear. In the world of information system management. There's always going to be connectivity between systems, between areas of information technology. With each other and you as an individual must be ready to adapt to the change or to the constant change of your career.

Examples of my preferred beginners training with career path

Welcome back. Welcome to this chapter where we are going to be talking about the integrating car part and information system management all through this Book, we have been talking about understanding the how and the why of information system management. As we wrap up on this Book now, let's bring everything together the world learned about it, about our careers into an integrative point of where you can actually start.

IT Networking Career Path for Beginners

Hi. In this session of integration. Of career part in the information system, management water. I believe by now you must have decided. That you want to go into networking and if you have not decided all. You are looking to the side. I will be talking about a networking part, starting with the recommended beginning Australian. In the past chapter, I've given the team to start with, come to it and come to applause. Once you are finished, come to a place, then you will have a better understanding of the beginner's software frameworks and the beginner software from after they come out and come to airplus training. You have an understanding of what a one is, a line Internet, Internet, duck net and so on.

Now, once you have this understanding within this country and come to the applause, you must have been introduced to the beginner's programming language either pow . Linas ilan CMT. The question is, do you need to know these picky programming languages? Do you need to know everything? And the answer is no. But my recommendation on the programming language for networking guys is always to start with power and also Linux. But they are all of the languages that you see there so that you can learn the process of computers and come to airplus. You are also introduced to CMT, which is a command line. And this is also used in Linux. Like I said, once you know how one or two works, you can leverage these skills on experience in other areas of the programming languages.

Then once you are done with your training income and come to a place, you can then start putting your resume together and getting yourself ready for the workforce. And these are some of the careers that you can pursue as a beginner in the networking space. You can start with communicating with others, depending on your background. Take, for example, in the past chapter for students that study communication or mass communication. You can look into becoming a communication analyst. Network specialists for those of us also studied communication, all the areas that imaging may join or other professionals. If you are done with Congemi and come to a plus for beginners, you should be able to go into the network as a specialist. There might be some training that you just need to take one or two four network specialists, like six and eight.

Maybe understanding how Cisco works or setting the platform works. And you can also go into I.T. specialist in the attic specialists. You can always search for these jobs. Look at what the requirements are and see what you've learned from your income to applause. And this programming and different walks. And they know what these jobs require. And you can tell your résumé towards them. And you can start applying for those jobs. And last but not least, you can also start your career as an I.T. MDX specialist. With an I.T. ethics specialist, you will be introduced to a server for the computer areas of information system management. But you will be able to function in this area if you have taken a computer and come to airplus trading. In the networking space. And if you have any questions. Please drop your comment in the comment chapter or send the instructor a message.

IT Programing Career Path for Beginners

Hi. In this chapter, I'm going to be talking about programming. If you have decided to go into programming or you're looking to go into programming, my recommended beginners training. Like I said in some previous chapters east of Star, we ishmail success in JavaScript. You also have the Piketon Vrba micro sequel. Do you have to learn all these? No, it all depends on the part you want to choose. If you have the bandwidth, you can. But you don't have to. Less classified. My recommended beginners training is a shameless yesses JavaScript. That is, if you're looking to go into a beginners career in things like Web development, Web designer. UX designer or anything that has to do with a Web framework. But if you are looking to go into a back room, walk maybe more of a data driven functionality in the programming space.

Good. I will recommend you look into Python, Vrba, Micro and sequel. Well, my recommendation is Vrba micro and sequel Wali. Those are my recommendations. Now, when you are taking the training in SeQual. You will definitely be introduced to the beginner software framework, such as Microsoft Database, Oracle Database, Progress Database, my sequel. Now you have to know all of these databases. The answer to that question is no. You just need to get trained, Iwon, and you can leverage your experience and your skill set in this environment into another database environment. 80 percent of the statements in these database environments are the same, but they are structured in the way you're either queries, Mobb, different.

Let's talk about the beginner's programming languages in the beginners programming language, like I said, HTML seesaws, JavaScript, Python, Vrba, Micron's sequel. You also have all the languages. But these are my beginner's recommendation languages. Now let's talk about the beginner's Curriers. If you're looking to go into anything that has to do with Web development, Web designing, you X, which is user interface or user extension interface designing, then the beginners recommend that training for you would be to take a training in HTML in JavaScript for a start as a Web developer, Web designer, USANA or UI designer.

Yeah, all the software coding that you need, PSB, dot net. These are the frameworks that you can use for Jangal. But for a starter, for a beginner, take on HTML, CSS and JavaScript training. Data analyst as developers. If you are looking to go into data analytics and secret development, then I recommend you start with a Vrba micro training and sequel. These two program languages will give you the starting point into data analytics and also sequel development. And these are my recommendations. You are all those beginner software training platforms that are out there into these what for Web developers? Things like Pauperized Djamila, you have Dreamweaver. And just to mention a few.

IT Software Career Path for Beginners

Hi. In this session, we're going to be talking about the software part of information system management. If you have decided to go into this part of Corio. Just to leverage a software application that I've viewed out there and see how you can start a career. In that software environment. Take, for example. In my introduction, I said I work as a consultant. SRP is a software application that is being used by Fortune 500 companies. For that day to day businesses. I Learned how to use the application, and I became a consultant in that environment. So my recommended starting point on my recommended beginner straightening point is for you to learn one programming language.

One software. It's always good. Most especially, you have to learn one software application. If we're able to land two, three, that's great. But one software is always good, and when it comes to programming, if you want to learn programming, that's also good. But we're going to talk about what type of program you have to learn. You don't have to be a programmer. The beginner's software framework is this. Microsoft's office is very important. If you're looking to go into this software, part of information system management, you have to learn the maps of Microsoft Excel and maps of PowerPoint, how to use those tools, because they are very, very important for management presentations and management work.

Now, there are several databases out there that have several ERP systems out there, and they have CRM systems that are out there. OK, let's take an example and make it Pratico. When I sell Leinwand software. What I mean is you can learn one ERP system, how it works. Example, you can learn how. Microsoft is dynamic. All you can learn is how HP walks. Or you can learn how one CRM works, let's say OSIS force system. If you learn one ERP system or any CRM system or database, like I always say, you can always leverage the skill that you learned from one into another. The beginner's programming languages. I'll recommend Vrba, Michael. Sequel. I scale and have no sequel.

Do you have to know all of these beginner's programming languages? No. All you have to do is decide to let one. Or to. Well, I recommend it. Programming language is always a sequel. All Veber. Michael. Well, you have to understand that it all depends on the field you want to start your career with. The beginner's courier for software. He's a business analyst. You can start your career as a business analyst. As a business analyst, what will you need? You will need at least one software application to specialize in. And if you decide to take one programming language, you can take either Vrba Micro or you can take SeQual. That would be my recommendation.

When you are learning either this software or programming language. You will be introduced to the software frameworks of that application. You also our system analyst, as a system analyst, you are going to be working within a certain application. And that application is to the same thing, you have to learn how that application works. One of the things you always do before you start putting your resume out there is to look at these careers and look at the one that best suits you. Once you are done with your training. You can become a research analyst, a marketing analyst, an I.T. system auditor.

All of this Korea does not necessarily mean that you are cold. No, Codan is involved in the software space. Most of the software functionality is functional. All you need to do is learn one or two applications. Maybe one programI. But most importantly, the beginner software, the Microsoft suite, then one database, one ERP system. If you don't want to do an ERP system now, you can land a CRM system. And if you have an equation, always feel free to message an instructor and will be able to give you feedback.

www.ingramcontent.com/pod-product-compliance
Lightning Source LLC
Chambersburg PA
CBHW072054230526
45479CB00010B/1065